SELLING IT RIGHT!

Getting Results With Integrity

Michelle Correia Templin

The  Company

Helping organizations achieve success through Ethical
Leadership and Values-Based Business Practices

To order additional copies of this handbook, or for information on
other WALK THE TALK® products and services,
contact us at
1.888.822.9255
or visit our website at
www.walkthetalk.com

SELLING IT RIGHT!

Inquiries regarding permission for use of the material contained in this book should be addressed to:
The WALK THE TALK Company
2925 LBJ Freeway, Suite 201
Dallas, Texas 75234
972.243.8863

WALK THE TALK books may be purchased for educational, business, or sales promotion use.

WALK THE TALK® and The WALK THE TALK® Company are registered trademarks of Performance Systems
Corporation.

Printed in the United States of America
10 9 8 7 6 5 4 3 2 1

Edited by Steve Ventura and Michelle Sedas
Designed and Printed by MultiAd

ISBN 1-885228-65-1

51295

9 781885 228659

This book is dedicated to the memory of:

My father, Maurice – who taught me the meaning of respect, self-discipline, and appreciation for hard work.

and

My mother, Mary – who showed me how to live life with pizzazz!

CONTENTS

INTRODUCTION

"Our organization espouses the highest ethical standards,"

but …

"Sometimes I need to do whatever it takes to get the sale!"

You are a salesperson!

Your department is the heartbeat of your business, and your work is critical to your organization's success.

You want to succeed and feel good about what you do, and your organization is counting on you "to deliver." As a result, there may be times when you find yourself torn between what seem to be two contradictory goals: selling as much as possible versus doing the right and noble thing.

Sound familiar? If so, this book is for YOU!

With corporate scandals on the cover of almost every newspaper and trade journal, it's not surprising that so many organizations have introduced extensive ethics training and integrated sound, fundamental values throughout the workplace. However, there still is confusion (and some skepticism) when it comes to promoting an ethical culture within the sales group. And much of that confusion rests in the minds of salespeople, themselves.

The fact is, far too many people in sales fail to understand the nature and essence of their own profession. They see it as a bounty to acquire rather than a process to follow ... an end unto itself rather than a means to a larger end. Ergo, the all-too-common misconception that "sales" and "ethics" are mutually exclusive concepts. In reality, however, nothing could be further from the truth. Meeting sales goals and operating with integrity are NOT "either/or" propositions – they're complimentary ones. And that's GREAT news for all of us!

As you know, targets, goals, and quotas will always be components of our business – and much of the time, they're not of our own choosing. What *is* our choice, however, is *how* we approach those goals ... how we meet them. And it's absolutely critical that we choose the very best means to accomplish the ends we seek.

To those who wonder how they can improve their sales results and overall job satisfaction, I say READ ON! The pages that follow will provide clarity and guidance – perhaps reinforcing what, deep down, you've felt all along.

Throughout this work, you'll be exposed to what may be a new way of thinking about your sales career … a new definition for salesmanship. Apply what you read, and you'll never have to choose between a profitable selling career and a noble, ethical one.

You *can* have both. You *should* have both. You WILL have both by …

Selling It Right!

A person of character takes as much trouble to discover what is right as the lesser man takes to discover what will pay.

~ Confucius

REMEMBER THAT CHARACTER COUNTS!

What are the most critical qualities for a salesperson to possess in order to have a successful career? Quite often, the answer to this question includes responses such as, "outgoing personality," "aggressiveness," or "the gift of gab." But what about honesty, trustworthiness, sincerity, and integrity? How often do they make the list?

Unfortunately, at one time or another, each of us has figuratively walked into a "used car lot" and experienced the process of manipulation. Many of us have been *sold* something we later regretted buying. Rarely do we go back to the same seller for a second beating. We've all learned from experience to be very cautious around salespeople.

This creates a pretty big challenge for an honorable salesperson. If every new buyer is afraid of being manipulated, he or she will have a hard time trusting you. However, you can break through this barrier by exhibiting high ethics and integrity. With values as your selling foundation, you can create "customers for life."

Developing Trust

Finding the appropriate balance between persistence and patience is important in order to enjoy an honorable and successful sales career. You are most valuable to your organization when you have the patience to develop long-term relationships with your customers. In order to do that, you need to be trustworthy and reliable. Successful selling occurs when you and your customer trust each other.

Because there are many self-centered salespeople in the business world today, your customer's first assessment of you might be negative – simply because he or she believes you are trying to force a sale. How refreshing it will be for this customer to encounter someone of character who truly cares about his or her needs instead of just chalking up another sale.

But good character and trustworthiness are not qualities that you can simply tell people you possess. The only way your customer will believe you have these qualities is by seeing you *demonstrate* them!

When calling on a customer, think about what you would want from a salesperson. Most likely your list would include honesty, trustworthiness, knowledge, optimism, and sincerity. You want salespeople of great character. And here's how you can be one of them:

Be Forthcoming

One of the biggest complaints of buyers is that they are not sure what the salesperson who calls on them wants. This alone can lead to mistrust. Often, the customer is concerned about being tricked into a purchase that he or she will later regret.

You can eliminate that barrier by being forthcoming. Always let your customer know *who* you are and *why* you are making contact:

> *"My name is Jim Smith and I am a sales representative for XYZ Copiers. I would like to ask you about your current copier to determine if another copy solution might benefit you and your company. May I ask you a couple of questions?"*

In ten seconds, you can tell your customer who you are, whom you represent, and what your goal is for the conversation. This is a helpful and courteous thing to do. It's a great way to demonstrate your professionalism and begin a trusting, win-win relationship.

Be Truthful

Lying is often a gut-level, defensive reaction to perceived danger. You may be tempted to stretch or manipulate the truth in order to create a more favorable impression on your customer. *But will you?*

Most people can sense when someone isn't completely honest with them. If you feel a need to hide the truth, take a moment and think about how you would benefit from a more trusting relationship. Compare that to the short-term gain you *might* get by evading the truth.

Keep Your Promises

Your reputation as a trustworthy salesperson will be built by doing what you say you are going to do. Customers need to know they can count on you. They expect you to keep your commitments.

Certainly, it's important to make customers happy. But unfortunately, for some salespeople this means promising things they really aren't sure they can do. Don't succumb to that temptation. Your word must be your bond.

If you say you will drop off a sample at three o'clock, do it! If you aren't sure you will have the sample ready by three, don't make that commitment. Instead, let your customer know you will get back with him or her to confirm an accurate delivery time. If you say you will check the status of an order, do it! Then report back promptly – even if the news isn't what the person wants to hear.

Your customers are relying on you. They need to have confidence in your ability to provide the information they need to do their jobs. Keeping your promises is how you build trust and demonstrate integrity.

Be There ... and Show You Care

Another common sales mistake is being readily available to close a deal and take the order – but not available to solve problems once the transaction has concluded. Customers need your attention and compassion *after* the sale as well. Not every transaction is going to go smoothly. How you handle glitches during and after the sale is another demonstration of your professionalism.

It's no secret that customers have choices. They can choose to buy from you or from your competitors. When you demonstrate high ethics and integrity, you increase your chances of becoming (and staying) the vendor of choice.

Contrived techniques intended to manipulate customers are ineffective. The best thing you can do is to be trustworthy, forthcoming, truthful, reliable, and client-focused. Not only will this improve your relationship with your customer, it will also enhance your ability to make a sale. Even more importantly, it will make it easier to acquire quality referrals down the road.

Always maintain the highest ethical standards and be true to your character. This is the very best thing you can do for your customers, for your organization, and for yourself.

Opportunity may knock only once,
but temptation leans on the doorbell.

~ Anonymous

TURN TEMPTATIONS INTO TRUST

Throughout your sales career, there will be times when you're tempted to behave less than ethically. Giving into those temptations will not only add stress to your life, it will also negatively impact your sales results. Let's face it, as a salesperson you probably have a "longer leash" than many of your peers in other departments. Most likely, you also have a tremendous amount of pressure to hit your sales goals. And you will encounter opportunities to obtain your goals through inappropriate means.

Here are some of the most common temptations for salespeople:

- Making promises or commitments that cannot be met in order to make the sale.

- Stretching the truth or withholding information that would negatively affect a sale.

- Overcharging or selling an inappropriate product to gain a higher commission.

- Conducting personal business on company time.

- Accepting gifts or favors from clients trying to gain preferential pricing.

Temptations to make unethical choices will not decrease as your career progresses. In fact, they will increase as you raise the bar on your goals and expectations. Overcoming these temptations is how you display character. It won't necessarily happen overnight. It will take hard work and determination to stay the course.

Temptation Triggers

Watch out for "The Big Four." These are the primary factors leading to unethical behavior:

GREED

The drive to acquire more and more in one's self-interest.

SPEED

The motivation to cut corners in response to the warp pace of business.

LAZINESS

Taking the easy path of least effort and resistance.

HAZINESS

Acting and reacting without thinking.

Check Yourself Out!

Self-evaluation is a critical component of an ethical selling career. Of course, you will continue to fine tune your sales skills as your career progresses. As you do that, it is also important to periodically examine and reflect on your behaviors to ensure you're conducting yourself with the highest integrity. Complete the **Salesperson's Ethics Self-Assessment** on the following page to help identify your integrity strengths and developmental opportunities.

SALESPERSON'S ETHICS SELF-ASSESSMENT

(Circle "Y" for yes or "N" for no)

In the last six months, have I ...

Y – N   Lied or manipulated the truth to make a sale?

Y – N   Conducted personal business on company time?

Y – N   Accepted gifts or gratuities in exchange for favors?

Y – N   Used or taken company resources for personal purposes?

Y – N   Called in sick when I really wasn't?

Y – N   Misrepresented how I spent company time?

Y – N   Fudged an expense sheet, sales call log, or other report?

Y – N   Used an ethically derogative term when referring to someone?

Y – N   Engaged in negative gossip regarding customers or coworkers?

Y – N   Snooped into a customer's or coworker's private conversation?

Y – N   Knowingly ignored an organizational rule or procedure?

Y – N   Knowingly failed to follow through on something I said I would do?

Y – N   Withheld information that others needed?

Y – N   Taken or accepted credit for a sale that I did not earn?

Y – N   Failed to correct or admit to a mistake?

Y – N   Knowingly let someone screw up and get into trouble?

Earning Trust

Being an ethical salesperson has its challenges. But you make it easier if you choose, upfront, to do it right. Telling "little white lies" to your customers to get the sale is wrong! Being less than forthcoming with your employer about how you spent your sales day is wrong! Eliminate such temptations by choosing to be consistently honest with everyone you work for and serve.

Customers care about your level of integrity as much as anything else. Never risk tarnishing your reputation by making an unethical choice. *The only way to gain trust is to behave in a trustworthy manner at all times!* True character is displayed when you do the right thing – no matter the consequences.

EXPECT ETHICAL DILEMMAS

Many sales professionals *say* they want to be ethical. But merely stating your desire will not make you an ethical salesperson. You see, ethics "happens" when good beliefs are translated into good behaviors. Without the action part, all you have are good intentions.

Most of the time, when reaching an ethical crossroads, you will know the right thing to do. However, there may be moments when you want to *sell yourself* on making an unethical decision. That's when you need to assess your priorities ... that's when you need to ask yourself:

What should I do to be the most successful salesperson I can be?

Obviously, the answer to that question depends upon your definition of "success." For truly ethical sales professionals, the answer is simple: Real success means selling with integrity ... doing the right and honorable thing. Salespeople who meet their quotas using unethical tactics rarely, if ever, enjoy lasting success. When you obtain your goals by cheating, you deny yourself the feeling of honest accomplishment.

Keep true, never be ashamed of doing right; decide on what you think is right and stick to it.

~ George Eliot

The Ethical Action Test

Taking The Ethical Action Test is a great way to check your decisions for "rightness" before you act. Use the questions below (or similar ones supplied by your organization) as your litmus test. Answering "no" to one or more of the following would suggest the need to rethink your situation – or to seek additional counsel and advice.

THE ETHICAL ACTION TEST

A. Is it legal?
B. Does it comply with our rules and guidelines?
C. Is it in sync with our organizational values?
D. Will I be comfortable and guilt-free if I do it?
E. Does it match our stated commitments and guarantees?
F. Would I do it to my family and friends?
G. Would I be perfectly okay with someone doing it to me?
H. Would the most ethical person I know do it?

© Performance Systems Corporation. Reproduced with permission.

Sales, by its very nature, is a competitive field. Obviously, you are expected to get results for your organization and for your customers. But you are also expected to get those results legally and ethically. If you allow yourself to lose sight of this, you jeopardize your reputation, your relationship with your customers and coworkers, and your sales career.

Never be willing to sacrifice your integrity for short-term gain. Avoid the trap of justifying inappropriate behavior with statements such as:

"How else can I reach my sales goal?"
"Everyone else does it!"
"They expect me to do that!"
"The boss does it!"
"No one will know!"
"Some rules were meant to be broken!"
"That's sales!"

While such rationalizations may be conscience-soothing, they don't change the fact that wrong is wrong – regardless of how you try to spin it.

Right vs. Right

Occasionally, you will face "ethical dilemmas" – times when instead of having to choose between right and wrong, you find yourself torn between two apparent rights. This is the most difficult ethical challenge: managing competing rights. Competing rights are issues that need to be thought through, talked through, and worked through.

You know you have the potential for an ethical dilemma when you use the words "but it's also right to … " Here are some examples:

It's right to get the business for your company, *but it's also right to* be honest with your customer.

It's right to be a driven and assertive salesperson, *but it's also right to* respect the territories and boundaries set within your organization.

It's right to earn the highest commission available, *but it's also right to* sell the product that best suits your customer's needs.

It's right to make your customer happy, *but it's also right to* stay within the rules and guidelines of your organization.

It's right to respect information given to you in confidence, *but it's also right to* report violations of laws and ethical standards.

The absolute best advice for anyone facing a sales dilemma of competing rights is **Get Help!** These situations are the most difficult things you will have to deal with throughout your career. They can take a big toll on you. So, seek counsel from whatever resources are available within your organization. An objective point of view can be invaluable in deciding what's *more* right when there are no apparent wrongs.

Don't *sell yourself* on doing the wrong thing. Your reputation will be built around the choices you make. When facing an ethical dilemma, make the right choice!

DO YOUR HOMEWORK

There are no shortcuts when preparing for a successful sales career. You have to do your homework. You need to know your products, your customers, your competitors, and your profession. Really knowing your business demonstrates a commitment to your job and enhances your personal credibility.

There are no secrets to success. It is the result of preparation, hard work, and learning from failure.

~ Colin Powell

Know Your Products

Take the initiative for learning everything you can about your organization's products and services. For example ...

◆ Stay familiar with all of the brochures, announcements, and advertisements released by your organization. Read industry related publications available at your workplace. Spend time observing your manufacturing and distribution operations whenever possible.

◆ Practice communicating technical knowledge and complex aspects about your products in a way that will make it easier for customers to understand. Be prepared to answer questions regarding small details about your products – as well as the history and evolution of your organization.

- ◆ Sign up for any available classes that will provide a greater awareness of your industry. Maintain your knowledge about the laws and regulations that pertain to what you do. Remember: If you want to be treated like a knowledgeable sales professional, you have to be one!

People want to know they are dealing with an expert. Your product and industry knowledge can be the determining factor when it comes to a customer making a buying decision. Not only will your increased knowledge help you assist your customer, it will also provide you with greater self-confidence.

Know Your Customers

A professional salesperson always takes time to research the company or person he or she is about to call on. It is important to know the company's history, number of employees, annual sales, recent or potential mergers, etc. Anything you can find out about the organization is valuable information for you. Being knowledgeable about your customer shows that you respect and care about him or her.

The best preparation for tomorrow is to
do today's work superbly well.

~ Sir William Osler

Thorough preparation before every sales call is what will set you apart from your competitors.

26

Most sales experts recommend that you create a rapport with your customer in order to establish a relationship. What better way to do this than to discuss what you have learned about his or her organization? You can find much of the information you need by researching national and local newspapers, trade publications, and the internet – as well as reviewing the organization's Annual Report.

Things like the company's mission and philosophies, recent mergers, or changes in executives could be pertinent to the purchase of your product and therefore are appropriate to discuss at the beginning of a sales call. Doing that also says a lot about your dedication and professionalism. It's a great way to begin a sincere and trusting relationship. This is especially true for the first couple of encounters with a new client.

Down the road, as your relationship with your customer solidifies, you will want to know about his or her family and hobbies. But addressing them in the beginning can be problematic. The customer may feel as though you are trying to manipulate a sale. As an ethical and honorable salesperson, you should never manipulate your customer. Instead, your goal should be to assist the person in making a good purchasing decision that will end up benefiting your client and his or her company.

Know Your Competition

Knowing how your competitors operate can make or break a sale for you. How else can you accurately advise your customer unless you have thorough knowledge of your industry? If you fail to research and study your industry, you are doing yourself and your customers a disservice. You can't possibly sell effectively if you are presenting your product with a limited amount of information.

Regularly call or visit your competitors to get a feel for what customers are being presented. Study the competition's websites and literature for valuable comparisons with yours.

When researching your competition, ask yourself the following questions:

- What advantage does your company offer over the competition?

- What do your competitors provide that you do not?

- How do your competitors' product features compare to yours?

- How does your competitors' customer service compare to yours?

Make a list of the pros and cons of each organization. This will help you anticipate some of your customer's potential concerns. By anticipating possible objections, you can prepare your responses and have a better chance of overcoming them.

Know Your Profession

You are a salesperson. This means you should also study salesmanship! Stay abreast of the latest techniques on negotiating. Keep reading! Continue to refine your communication and listening skills. Continue to critique yourself and be open to feedback from others. Keep improving! And as you do, remember to stay focused on your values and your integrity. Never stop learning about sales!

COMMUNICATE EFFECTIVELY

Effective communication is a major contributing factor to our overall success in life. And that's especially true for sales professionals. It is imperative that you communicate clearly and effectively.

> *The biggest problem in communication is the illusion that it has been accomplished.*
>
> ~ George Bernard Shaw

Most people consider communication to be just the *words* that we say. However, communication is much more than that. We communicate not just by our words, but also by our tone of voice, our body language, our choice of attire, our written correspondence, and a lot more. In fact, experts say that on average only seven percent of our communication is done through our words; thirty-eight percent comes from our tone of voice, and a whopping fifty-five percent through our body language. That means that most communication with your customers occurs without you saying a word!

Nonverbal Communication

Here are some of the nonverbal ways you communicate to, and with, your customers:

1. **Attire and Personal Appearance.** Take an honest look at your overall professional appearance. What does your choice of attire and style say about you? What would you like it to say? Fashion trends are great for socializing but may not reflect an appropriate image to your customers. Un-

less you are selling fashion, the best rule of thumb is to stay conservative. The impression you want to give is one of professionalism. You want your clients to remember *you*, not your attire. Avoid wearing clothes and accessories that draw attention and take away from your sales message.

When preparing to visit a customer ...

- Make sure your clothes are clean and pressed.

- Keep shoes and leather briefcases or bags polished.

- Make sure your presentation materials are organized and neat.

- Check your fingernails and hair for neatness.

- Avoid distracting jewelry, accessories, and excessive makeup.

- Keep your car clean and organized – just in case your client walks you out or asks that you drive to lunch.

Remember that your appearance affects the "first impression" you make. And how you are perceived affects the way your customers will interact with you. What does your appearance "communicate" to your customers? You want your clients to think of you as professional, ethical, and trustworthy. Keep that in mind when preparing for your next sales call.

2. Body Language. Your body language will speak louder than your words. So, what you say will have either more or less impact depending upon your tone, inflection, and mannerisms.

Begin with a smile. With few exceptions, customers prefer to do business with warm, friendly people who are interested in serving. A sincere smile goes a long way in communicating your desire to work with your client.

If you are new to sales, you may be nervous about your presentation. A friendly smile, followed by a warm greeting, is a great way to steady your nerves. But don't stop there. Extend a firm and confident handshake. Maintain a self-assured posture. Keep your chin up and don't fidget! Observe the position of your arms. Are they closed and defensive, or open and inviting?

Look 'em in the eyes! It's been said that "the eyes are the mirror of the soul." Our eyes reflect our emotions and thoughts. Eye contact provides insight as to our attitudes and self-confidence. So, look directly at your customer when speaking.

3. Vocal Tone, Pitch, and Pace. The pitch and volume of your voice also affect how you are perceived. If you are too loud, you can reflect an overbearing or pompous attitude. If you are too soft-spoken, you may project a sense of insecurity.

Honest self-assessment, here, is very helpful. However, we can become so accustomed to how we sound that it may be hard to evaluate ourselves. Ask others for constructive feedback regarding your vocal pitch and volume. Regularly record and play back your phone conversations to assess how you sound. And be sure to evaluate your pace of speaking. When nervous or excited, salespeople often speed up their speaking pace. That's something you definitely need to avoid. Make sure you emit a calm and confident demeanor.

Don't allow frustration or anger to enter into your communication style. This won't help you or your customer. If you remind yourself that your goal is to serve your customer, it will be easier to keep your cool.

If you feel angry or frustrated, take a deep breath and count to ten. Then, try to clearly articulate your concerns in a way that will enhance your selling efforts.

Not only is it important to be conscious of your own nonverbal communication, it is critically important to be alert to your customer's as well. Like you, customers will provide their own nonverbal cues. And learning how to read those cues is critical to your selling success.

4. Written Correspondence. The last form of nonverbal communication is written correspondence. With the increasing use of e-mail, how you write is becoming more and more relevant for success as a sales professional. Here are some things to keep in mind:

- ◆ Make sure your written correspondence is clear and concise. Separate your thoughts so they are easy to understand. Use bullet points in proposals to distinguish significant areas. Keep your paragraphs short. And, eliminate slang (okay) or words with double meanings (cool!).

- ◆ Don't use e-mail to communicate something that would be better relayed in person. Especially when delivering bad news, have the courage to share information with your clients directly. They will respect you for it.

- ◆ With few exceptions, handwritten correspondence is only appropriate for thank you notes. Such notes should be neat, brief, and sincere expressions of gratitude.

◆ Summarizing your sales presentations and important conversations in writing is good business practice. Doing so helps to eliminate misunderstanding and confusion which may eventually lead to hard feelings.

Verbal Communication

Of course, along with our nonverbal messages, we also use words. And they can either help or hinder our ability to sell effectively. Think before you speak! Everything you say affects your sales outcome.

In order to improve your verbal communication ...

Keep It Simple. Choose words that are explicit and unambiguous. Your customer should not have to figure out what you mean. Be straightforward. Get to the point! Express yourself honestly and openly. And by all means, make it brief!

Verify and Clarify. Never assume you know what your customer is saying. Verify by repeating (or rephrasing) what you heard.

Occasionally you'll sense that a customer is either holding something back or has a concern that he or she is unable to verbalize. When that occurs, help him or her get it out on the table. If you feel something has been left unsaid, do your best to surface it. Of course, you will need to use tact and diplomacy when communicating your "gut feelings":

I sense that something is concerning you. Tell me about it.

I feel you're somewhat hesitant about moving forward. I'd really like to hear any concerns you may have.

No "Buts!" When you want to add to what your customer has said, get in the habit of using "and" instead of "but." "But" negates what was said previously. "And" or "as well" will help your statement be in addition to what your customer said:

> *I hear your concern about the price – (no but here) – and I also know the quality is important to you.*

This small change implies you are a partner rather than an adversary.

Deal With Reality. Many salespeople avoid uncovering "unspoken messages" because they do not want to address the real issues. They would rather pretend that everything is fine. Never avoid surfacing the truth. Avoiding issues is a disservice to everyone involved. The best time to learn about your customer's fears or concerns is NOW!

You shouldn't have to guess about someone's intentions or implications. If you are unsure about the customer's state of mind, ASK! You will gain credibility for not having assumed his or her intent. (You'll find more on this in the next chapter.)

Don't Talk Too Much! At times – either due to their egos or insecurities – salespeople feel the need to speak much more than they should. The fact is, you can provide *too many* features and *too many* benefits ... just *too much* information. Stay in tune with your customers. Are they asking for more details or do they seem restless and uninterested?

Remember that when it comes to speaking, less is often more. It's much better to stay concise and wait for them to ask questions that pertain to their specific needs.

"COMMUNICATION KILLERS" ... TO AVOID

- ◆ Derogatory jokes, profanity, or abusive language.

- ◆ Irritating habits such as overusing "um" and "like."

- ◆ Technical jargon or industry acronyms that customers may be unfamiliar with.

- ◆ Indirect requests or mixed messages.

- ◆ Speaking negatively about your competition, coworkers, or other customers.

Finally, always remember that the most important thing that you can do to be an effective communicator is to be sincere. Let your good intentions shine through. If you care about your clients and treat them with the respect they deserve, you will communicate your integrity. And integrity is golden!

I attribute the little I know to my not having been ashamed to ask for information.

~ John Locke

HAVE THE COURAGE TO QUESTION

Asking the right questions is another way of demonstrating your professional integrity. Certainly, your presentation skills will be helpful down the road. But before you jump into your standard spiel, STOP ... and find out what your customer needs. Carefully considering the proper questions to ask prior to meeting with your client is good business practice. The more you know about your customer's situation, the better you can serve him or her. Buyers rarely want to hear about your product before you've inquired about their needs and any problems they may be facing.

My favorite comparison is that of a salesperson to a medical doctor. It would be pretty unreasonable if a doctor prescribed medication for you without asking several questions about your ailments. So, how can you help to "cure" the customer if you haven't bothered to ask about his or her "ailments"?

Questions should all have one goal in mind: obtaining information to help customers get what they want. Be as authentic as you can be. Be as sincere as possible. Be clear about why you are asking the questions:

> *"I have an unusual sales philosophy – I only sell to people who can benefit from my product. With that in mind, I'd like to ask you a few questions in order to determine if I can be of service."*

Use questions to create win-win relationships ... to help you and your customer determine if your product is a true solution to his or her problem.

Why Courage?

Often, a novice salesperson will hesitate to ask a question for fear of looking foolish. He or she might also be concerned about appearing overly intrusive. Just the opposite is true! When you avoid asking pertinent questions – ones that could help you better serve your customer – you are doing an injustice to everyone involved.

Asking questions takes courage. Why? Because you might not get the answer you want to hear. You may discover that your product is *not* the best solution to the customer's problem. As a professional salesperson, you must have the courage to ask the right questions to get to the bottom of your client's needs and determine the best "prescription." If your product isn't the best solution, you should point the customer in the right direction and refocus your energy on prospects who *have* a need for your services.

Spend time thinking about the questions that will help you gain the most insight from your customer. Prepare them in advance. Just keep in mind that you might not be able to determine the most effective questions until you're actually with the person.

Think about it. What do you need to know? First of all, you need to know if there is a problem or a need. You can find out by asking questions like:

What's the biggest challenge you are facing with your internal bookkeeping system?

What's kept you from using an outside company to maintain your landscaping?

How would you improve your current copier?

Notice that such questions cannot be answered with a simple "yes" or "no." This is helpful when trying to gather as much information as possible. Questions that cannot be answered with a yes or no are called open-ended questions – and they typically start with WHO, WHAT, WHERE, WHEN, WHY, or HOW.

Identify two open-ended questions that will help you determine if a customer has a problem you can solve:

1.

2.

After asking your initial question(s), follow up with more:

Who will be involved in the project?

How does that impact your company?

Where do you stand in relation to the purchase?

Why is it a problem for you?

What might be done to make you feel better about the situation?

When do you plan to make a decision?

Now take a separate piece of paper and create five to ten more questions that could help you better understand a customer's situation and needs.

Finally, practice asking the questions you have prepared. Make sure every inquiry helps you get a clearer picture of what your customer is facing.

Be Patient

After you ask a question, make sure you give the person time to respond. Many salespeople are uncomfortable with silence. As a result, they often answer questions for the customer. That's both presumptuous and rude.

Speaking of rude, I have observed many salespeople who ask a question and immediately follow with another one to fill the void. After you ask a question, allow the customer time to reflect on the answer. Have faith that he or she will answer if given a chance. And never assume you already know the answer. Not only does this show a lack of patience and professionalism, it also suggests you are more concerned about making a sale than meeting the customer's needs. So, listen to the *entire* answer. You may be surprised by what you uncover.

Use Diplomacy

If not asked properly, some questions may come across as impolite to the buyer. Preface a hard question with a soft introduction. Let them know your goal is to serve them:

> So that I can understand how to best help you, are you the sole decision maker, or will there be others involved in the purchasing decision?

*So that I can ensure I'd be able to support your timeline, when
do you want to make your purchase?*

Avoid Insulting Questions

Some sales "gurus" recommend that you ask questions that will force the
buyer to respond with an obvious "yes":

Isn't saving money important to you?

Don't you want to provide a more secure future for your family?

But these types of questions can insult your customer's intelligence. This
is a manipulation tactic that can result in you losing credibility. Be real!
Only ask questions that will help you assist your customer.

Once you have finished asking all of your critical questions, there is one
final question that must be answered by the buyer before you move on:

What else do I need to know in order to assist you?

Listening well is as powerful a means of communication and influence as to talk well.

~ John Marshall

LISTEN SO YOU CAN LEARN

In the previous chapter we discussed how critical it is to ask good questions. Of equal importance, however, is your ability to listen – really listen – to your customer's responses. Studies show that the average listener retains less than fifty percent of what he or she hears. If you are a poor listener, you are missing out on a large number of sales opportunities.

Most people think of themselves as good listeners. Interestingly enough, they also think most *other* people are *poor* listeners. The fact is, many conflicts in the workplace can be attributed to poor listening.

Being a good listener takes a tremendous amount of discipline and determination. There are several common listening challenges you should be aware of in order to improve your listening ability.

Roadblocks to Effective Listening

Lack of Discipline – You have a hard time staying focused on what your client is saying. Instead, your mind wanders and you begin planning what you'll say next while your client is talking.

Uncontrolled Passion – You are so eager and excited about your product, you interrupt before your customer can finish his or her statement. You stopped listening as soon as you sensed a sales opportunity.

Ego – You want to let your customer know you are smart and good at what you do. So, you do most of the talking – including telling the person what he or she needs.

Impatience – You simply do not want to wait to let your customer speak. In fact, the only thing you are actually listening for is the next opportunity to get a word in.

Assumptions – You assume you already know what your client is about to say, so you interrupt and finish his or her sentences.

Insecurity – You are afraid of either learning something you do not want to hear or forgetting a critical component to your "sales pitch." So, you stop listening and start worrying.

And worst of all …

Unconscious Habits – You are so accustomed to monopolizing conversations that it has become as natural as breathing. You are completely unaware of how you come across.

Stop Planning … Start Listening

Evaluate your own listening behaviors. How often do you catch yourself planning your next response instead of focusing on *everything* that is being said by your customer? The best way to control this habit is by making brief notes. As possible responses pop into your mind, write down one-word triggers to help you remember your thoughts later. Then immediately return your attention to what your customer is saying.

Customers Come First

This isn't just a customer service motto; it should be your listening paradigm. Because you're excited about a potential sale, you may be anxious to present your product or service. But you need to be patient. You will be evaluated by how attentive you are while your customer is speaking. Therefore, you should encourage your customer to expand by interjecting phrases such as: *Tell me more* and *Please expand.* This type of interactive listening *demonstrates* that you are paying attention.

Set the Stage

Creating the ideal listening environment is not always possible. Sometimes, you may be asked to make a quick presentation in a company lobby or hallway or to meet with your client in a noisy restaurant or coffee house. Listening is hard enough without the distractions that occur in these types of conditions.

Let your customer know you would prefer meeting in a quieter environment. However, if he or she declines to change locations, do what you can to eliminate distractions.

If you are meeting in a busy restaurant, stay away from tables by the window. Choose a quiet corner table and try to situate both of you so you're facing toward the least distracting view. Discipline yourself to mentally eliminate the distractions around you.

Listen and Learn

If you genuinely want to help customers make good purchasing decisions, you need to *learn* from them. By listening carefully, you will learn everything you need to best serve them.

To understand the power of listening is to take a lesson from nature. You have two ears and only one mouth. Listen twice as much as you speak. Even Mother Nature knows that

when you listen you learn.

DON'T MANIPULATE, NEGOTIATE!

Learning to negotiate properly can be a significant challenge for anyone who wants to sell with integrity. A professional salesperson's job is to encourage and influence a purchasing decision that will benefit the buyer – not to deceive the buyer into doing something he or she doesn't want to do. As an ethical salesperson, you never want to manipulate anyone into doing something that is not in his or her best interest, but you do want to encourage a sale that will be beneficial to the buyer. In order to help a customer make the best decision, you may need to negotiate some parts of the transaction.

To negotiate means that two parties bargain to reach an agreement. Negotiation has the best chance to succeed if both parties are seeking a win-win outcome. If either party has an "*I must win*" attitude, that person will most likely resort to manipulation to get his or her way.

How do you know the difference between healthy negotiation and inappropriate manipulation? If we persuade others to do what *we* want them to do – without any regard for what is in their best interest – we are manipulating. There are salespeople who achieve their sales goals using fear-based techniques and intimidation. We all have observed sellers taking advantage of confused customers. The people that resort to these tactics are not sales professionals – they're con artists!

As a salesperson, you have a moral responsibility – one that comes with your position. Selling is about serving … about helping your customers make buying decisions that will benefit them.

How *does* an ethical salesperson appropriately persuade a customer to buy? In order to answer this question we must reassess our selling paradigm. If you continue to think of your sales objective as one in which you do something *to* your customers instead of doing something *for* them, you are still heavily influenced by your own misconceptions about selling.

Five Selling Myths

Myth #1: Selling requires manipulation of the truth.

WRONG! Selling is <u>not</u> about deceiving – it's about *helping* people buy the right product. If you have to manipulate the truth to get the business, you have the wrong customer ... or the wrong product for that customer.

Always tell the truth – it's the easiest thing to remember.

~ David Mamet

You may feel pressure to be less than honest about your product or service in order to get the business. Fight it!

The single most important thing you can do is earn your customer's trust. You do that by being trustworthy. Unlearn any tactics that you have used in the past to orchestrate the contact. When you tell the truth, your integrity will shine through. And, your customers will open up and provide you with the information you need to help them buy.

Myth #2: Salespeople need to be super-competitive.

WRONG! Salespeople do not need to be competitive – they need to focus on their goals. Certainly, a little friendly competition between you and your peers can be fun and motivating. But don't become obsessed with winning. Looking over your shoulder to see what your peers have sold is a distraction from what you need to accomplish. Don't just strive to be the *top* salesperson on your team. Instead, focus on being the *best* salesperson you can be. *Everything else will fall into place.*

Work with your manager to set sales goals that are obtainable but will also stretch your skills. Create a plan to attack your goals. How many customers do you need to find per day? Per week? Per month?

Once you've created an ambitious plan, stay focused and stick with it! Don't get distracted by your colleagues' successes. Celebrate with them. More importantly, *learn* from them.

Myth #3: Salespeople need to be pushy in order to be successful.

WRONG! Salespeople need to be persistent, not pushy. There is a difference. If you are pushing someone to buy, you are not selling – you are intimidating.

Persistence in all of the following aspects of the sales cycle is critical to your success:

> *Developing the Relationship.* Your customer may make this harder on you than it needs to be – depending on the opinion he or she has about salespeople. Stick with it! Establishing authentic credibility and trust is the most important thing you can do for your sales success.

Identifying the Customer's Needs. Work hard to create the types of questions that will help you understand your customer's needs. Then work *even harder* to ask them in a way that will help the customer feel comfortable and respond with open, honest answers.

Presenting the Product. Be persistent when presenting your product. Let the customer know how much time it will take to make your presentation, and never go beyond the allotted time. Remember to tie every facet back to the needs and values of your client. Occasionally, customers may steer you off course with questions and concerns. Don't get your feathers ruffled. This is a good thing! It shows they're interested.

Gaining Commitment for the Purchase. This is where your persistence really pays off. You must give customers room to make decisions that they feel good about. However, your time is important, too. Don't hesitate to ask for a buying commitment. Think about how much easier this will be if you have created a trusting relationship up front.

Following Up for Referrals. The best time to ask for referrals is anytime! Be persistent in requesting referrals from your current customers. Remember, the best source of new business is your current business.

Myth #4: Successful salespeople are lucky.

WRONG! You might occasionally *feel* lucky, but consistent successful selling rarely happens due to luck. In reality, successful salespeople work very hard. They love what they do and they make it *look* lucky.

All of the successful salespeople I know are passionate about their product. They tout it to anyone who will listen. And, because they are always talking about their product, they run across more people who have a need for it. This isn't luck – it's the result of passion! The more people who know what you sell, the greater your chances of encountering someone who needs your product ... or knows someone who does.

Take your business cards with you everywhere. Be proud of what you do and the products you sell. Show your passion! Let people know you want to work with them.

"Lady Luck" is unreliable! Accomplished salespeople rely on passion, proactivity, and persistence.

Myth #5: To be successful, you must be a great "closer."

WRONG! Successful salespeople do not close anything! They leave every door open. They see additional opportunities with every customer rather than just the current transaction. They work at developing lasting relationships. They sell with integrity so they can go back to the same customer for more sales and referrals.

Don't focus on "closing the sale." Instead, focus on building a long-term relationship. Leave the door wide open for referrals. As an honorable salesperson, you'll have the luxury of revisiting your clients again and again because you've always behaved in an ethical and professional manner.

Remember that the *sale* is never *closed.* After you have obtained the first order, you will want to ask for additional sales and referrals. If you have behaved with integrity, this is a simple and natural thing to do.

Overcoming Objections

Overcoming objections is a normal part of negotiating a deal. If you are like most salespeople, you probably feel a bit of resentment when customers bring up reasons for *not* doing business with you. It takes a seasoned professional to realize that objections should not be feared. In fact, they are actually a sign that your customer is listening to you. When presented with an objection to your product or service, don't assume the sale is over. Objections are not "red lights." They don't have to end the sale. Try to think of them as "yellow lights." You will need to slow down and proceed with caution in order for the light to turn green again.

You may have been exposed to several "tricky" tactics for overcoming customer objections. Well, forget them! If you take a more honorable approach to selling, you will not need to resort to manipulative tactics. You simply need to acknowledge your customer's viewpoint and honestly express another perspective:

> Customer: *Your production capacity is not large enough!*

> Salesperson: *I understand how that might be a concern for you. Let me offer you another perspective so you can see how we will overcome this.*

Here, you might share a testimonial from another customer – explaining how he or she overcame the same issue. Or, you could present facts and figures that support your position.

Obviously, there are certain objections that you will hear with some frequency. Take, for example, the issue of pricing. This is a common concern. Customers want to be reassured they will be getting the most bang for their buck. Wouldn't you?

Prepare for price objections up front. Study your competition's pricing. Be ready to present and compare the features of your product that add value relative to the price:

Customer: *The price is too high!*

Salesperson: *Tell me more. What are you comparing it to? (By asking this question, you can determine whether the objection is serious or the customer just needs more assurance before purchasing.)*

Customer: *It just seems like a lot of money for a cellular phone!*

Salesperson: *I understand your feelings. It may help you to know that I have studied our competitor's pricing and I've found that ...*

The best way to overcome any objection is to prepare for it *before* you meet with the client. What would your concerns be if *you* were the buyer? Once you have determined the most likely objections, gather testimonials from other customers – or facts and figures that address the issues. By doing this in advance, you will speak with more confidence and authority. As a result, you'll gain credibility with your customer.

There will be times when you sense that your customer has a concern he or she is unwilling to share. This can be the hardest objection to overcome. Encourage your client to open up so you can address the issue:

I sense something is troubling you. Remember I am here to help. If we can get all of your concerns out on the table, I'm sure we'll be able to find the best solution, together.

Negotiate With a Clear Conscience!

Once you're sure that your product will benefit the customer, you should appropriately encourage him or her to buy. Don't be shy. Have fun with your presentation. Go for it! Do your best to create a positive and productive conclusion. As you negotiate remember to ...

- Focus on a *win-win* outcome.

- Present the features of your product – emphasizing how it will benefit the buyer.

- Overcome objections by calculating legitimate savings that will result from the purchase of your product.

- Share stories and testimonials from other satisfied customers.

- Prepare to address price objections with value-added responses.

- Ask the customer what it will take to gain his or her commitment, today!

- Express your passion for the product. Let the customer know why he or she should buy from you.

The Power of Persuasion

Good salespeople possess the natural ability to persuade others. Most of us learned the power of persuasion as children. At one time or another, we learned to persuade other kids to play the games we wanted to play. We persuaded our parents and siblings to do what we wanted to do. We have all been successful persuading teachers, supervisors, and ultimately customers to see things our way.

But, along with the ability to persuade comes a moral responsibility to respect the needs of others. Make sure you use your power of persuasion only to achieve good and noble results.

Focus on helping your customers get what *they* want, and you will eventually get what *you* want.

The greatest change in corporate culture,
and the way business is being conducted,
may be the accelerated growth of
relationships based on partnerships.

~ Peter Drucker

GET ON THE SAME SIDE
OF THE TABLE

Let's face it, there's a good chance that you won't be the only salesperson your client will speak to today. Buyers are inundated with vendors trying to sell their products. How will you distinguish yourself from your competition? What do you offer that your clients won't receive from anyone else?

In most cases, the product or service that you sell is *not* your distinguishing factor. This is a competitive marketplace, and buyers are looking for much more than just another vendor. Instead, these buyers are looking for salespeople who are willing to become *partners*.

Partnering occurs when two people or companies work together – sharing the risks and rewards of accomplishing a common goal. To partner with your clients means you not only sell a product that will meet their needs, but you also take the time to understand their objectives and help them achieve their overall goals.

Consider the physical image of being on the same side of the table. Normally, when you are presenting a product to a potential customer, you are on opposite sides of a desk or conference table. However, once the client's interest is sufficiently piqued or the sale is finalized, your customer may want to come around the desk and get on the same side of the table with you in order to work out the details. That's when you know a level of trust has been established and you both are now on the same team.

The value of creating a partnership cannot be overstated. Examine how you are offering partnerships to your clients. What specific things do you do to show you are willing, and able, to be on their team?

Here are a few examples of how you can "partner" with your customers:

◆ Offer references to other vendors – people you know and respect who provide additional products and services your customers need.

◆ Create a business newsletter that reviews insights or trends that you discover throughout the industry.

◆ Organize networking opportunities for your customers such as "Users Conferences," "Customer Colleges," and other initiatives designed to bring people together around a common interest.

◆ Ask your customers to be part of an advisory board that tests products and services prior to going to market. Solicit their feedback up front so you can better serve them down the road.

◆ Establish a *Business Book-of-the-Month Club* and invite your clients to join for continual professional development and networking.

◆ E-mail or send industry related articles to your clients.

◆ Inquire about their corporate charitable fundraising events and offer your support. You can become partners with your customers in doing good deeds for your communities, too.

In order to encourage a partnering atmosphere with your client, remember to ask questions that trigger "big-picture" responses – ones that show you are interested in more than just making a sale:

I would like to get a feel for your organization's priorities. What are the major challenges your organization is facing this year? What are your key business goals?

Let your customer know that you are interested in creating and maintaining more than just a buyer-to-seller relationship:

I value your business and I see my role in our relationship as much more than just your vendor. I see myself as your partner. I am committed to your overall success.

Here are a few personal examples of salespeople "partnering" with me rather than just selling me a product or service:

Investing in My Success

Normally investment brokers just help their clients invest their money. My broker did much more than that. He took the time to learn about my business. He asked questions to uncover my professional goals. Then, he used his connections to help get me on a local radio show to talk about my company. By doing this, he demonstrated his concern for the future of my business. I knew I had a partner who sincerely cared about my success. You can be sure I continue to give him my additional investment business … and I refer others to him as often as I can.

Banking Bliss

Another exceptional salesperson is my banker. Every time I meet with him, he asks me about my business. He takes a genuine interest in the specifics of my training programs, what companies I am working with, what topics are generating the most interest, etc. I even received a message from him while I was giving a keynote presentation wishing me success on the event. He sends me articles on the training industry, as well as relevant areas of the banking world. I know he cares about my professional success and my personal fulfillment. Therefore, I care about his. I refer clients to him as often as possible.

Retail Reality

You can exhibit a desire to be a partner in a retail environment as well. I bought a bottle of fragrance at Nordstrom many months ago. I later received a handwritten card from the salesperson thanking me for the purchase.

I happened to go by the same counter several months later. I mentioned to the salesperson that I was no longer using the perfume because it gave me a headache. She offered to take it back – but I was embarrassed to do so because it had been a long time since I made the purchase. She continued to insist and I finally agreed to think about it. Later that week, I received a handwritten card reminding me to return it. Her note demonstrated that she really cared about my happiness. She wanted to make sure I would not hesitate to buy from her again.

I finally returned the bottle of perfume. That very same day I purchased several additional items that I brought to her counter so she would receive credit for the sale. Just recently, I received a card from her advising me of an upcoming sale. Who do you think I will buy from? I look forward to bringing her my business because I know she can be trusted to do the right thing.

Building Customer Loyalty

Building a partnership creates customer loyalty. And fostering loyalty involves a commitment of heart as well as resources. It takes energy, time, and focus. The salespeople that commit to creating partnerships with their clients excel in sales. They aren't just committed to their clients – their clients are also committed to them! These types of customers not only return again and again, but they also bring more customers with them.

My goal in sailing isn't to be brilliant
or flashy in individual races;
it's just to be consistent over the long run.

~ Dennis Connor

GET OFF THE ROLLER COASTER

For many salespeople, the sales arena is like an amusement park roller coaster ride. There are lots of ups and lots of downs. Riding the roller coaster means your sales volume is inconsistent. When sales are up, you're on top of the world. When sales are down, you have to work from scratch to get them going again. This can be demoralizing for you and frustrating for your company.

The most common complaint I hear from sales managers is that their people do not understand the value of a *consistent* sales pipeline. Because salespeople tend to be passionate in nature, they often focus on current negotiations – channeling all of their energy in a single direction. Therefore, they often put off prospecting for new buyers, and rekindling old ones, until it is too late.

As a professional, you must be able to project who you will be selling to this month and next month … and every month after that. You are expected to continually cultivate new leads and maintain a consistent revenue stream for your business.

From "NO" to "GO"

A good way to improve your selling effectiveness is by categorizing all of your contacts. Doing that helps ensure that your efforts will be spread appropriately within each category. Some organizations will make this easier by providing customer maintenance software programs. If such a resource is not available, you'll need to create your own system.

I find it helpful to place clients into one of four categories:

"NO" – These people do not have a need for my product and are not likely to provide me with referrals.

"GROW" – These are new contacts. They are not completely familiar with my product or service. I have not established a solid relationship with them. I believe they might have a need I can satisfy, and I want to arrange a time, in the near future, to complete a needs analysis.

"SLOW" – I have met with these clients (face-to-face or over the phone), and they have a need for my product or service. They are unable to buy right now, but I believe they will purchase in the future. We have an established relationship. They could also be a good source of referrals.

"GO" – These customers are buyers. They have purchased in the past and will most likely buy again and/or refer other potential clients to me.

As you categorize *your* clients, it should become obvious how you need to spend your time. Here are some things to remember about time allocation:

Sorting the Wheat From the Chaff

If you know that a person does not have a need (or desire) for your product or service, and they will not be a viable source of referrals, you should place them into a different database or file cabinet. Salespeople often struggle with this because they want their territory or database to appear big, they want to look busy, or perhaps they are just really uneasy about giving up on a contact. However, purging contacts is absolutely necessary in order to maximize your time and energy.

I do not recommend that you completely delete "NO" files. Every once in a while, a "NO" customer will call you from out of the blue and expect you to remember conversations from the past. So you'll need to be able to access his or her file information. You should, however, take these people out of your working database. This will help you avoid dedicating time and effort to individuals who offer little in the way of sales potential.

10 – 10 – 10

The GROW, SLOW, and GO categories are very important. You need *all* of them to have consistent sales results. Make a habit of calling at least **10** contacts from each of these three categories every day. Even if you're busy finalizing the details of a large purchase, you need to maintain a presence with the other categories in your database.

The discipline it takes to balance your contacts is what separates good salespeople from great ones. Great salespeople know that, when a deal is finalized, they will need to have other pending opportunities. They spend at least one hour every day generating new business. They apply the energy and emotion they gain from making a sale to initiating new contacts or scheduling appointments with prospects. This way, they guarantee a more consistent sales pipeline.

The 80/20 Rule

Undoubtedly, you will have several customers who continue to buy from you on a regular basis. Eighty percent of your business will typically come from twenty percent of your customers. Many salespeople refer to this twenty percent as their "customer base." The people in this exclusive group need to feel valued and appreciated.

Maintaining your customer base is another fundamental responsibility of your profession. Regular follow up is critical. If you do not maintain your current customer base, your competition will! NEVER take customers for granted.

Don't Forget the "Little Guy"

Customers who do not buy in large quantities are no less important than those who do. These smaller customers know they're not big buyers. However, they still expect (and deserve) to be given respect and attention. Remember: Even if they never increase their order, small buyers could become your best source of referrals.

Save the Roller Coaster Ride for the Amusement Park!

Being an ethical salesperson means you are consistent. If you have had a reputation for being inconsistent in the past, change your ways today! You need to understand the importance of balancing your customers and your daily responsibilities. Make a commitment to develop new contacts every day. This takes discipline and professionalism. It takes devotion. You can do it!

SELL TO A DIVERSE CUSTOMER BASE

As a professional salesperson, not only must you understand the different features and benefits of your products, you must also understand (and appreciate) the differences in your customers.

This is a "global" economy. And that means that opportunities may arise for you to work with customers from around the world. Therefore, it's essential that you learn to respect different personality types as well as different cultures, religions, genders, and generations.

Cultural Differences

Most organizations today serve an ethnically diverse customer base. It will be essential for you to embrace cultural diversity. In most cases, working with different cultures is effortless. In fact, learning about different customs and traditions is fun. However, it is also easy for negative stereotypes and hidden assumptions to get in the way of working together productively. This is not only bad for your sales career; it's also bad for humanity.

Language Barriers

Occasionally you may work with someone who is difficult to understand because English is not his or her primary language. Your client may speak with a heavy accent or use a translator. Patience will play an important role in this situation. Make sure you do not rush through your conversations.

Speak clearly and slowly – and avoid using slang or colloquialisms. Phrases such as "a hop, skip, and a jump away" or "twenty-four/seven" can put more strain on an already difficult interaction. Choose your words carefully. Use verbiage that is simple and easy to understand. Your customer may require extra time to think about what you are saying. Put yourself in his or her shoes. Be compassionate!

When dealing with a language difference, it's wise to summarize the conversation in writing. This will allow your customer to review what was said and be better prepared to make a decision.

Never try to rush anyone into buying. Make sure he or she understands all aspects of the deal. Ask clear and direct questions, and wait patiently for the answers. Rephrase or repeat what your customer says to ensure you understand it correctly. Ask your customer if he or she has any concerns or needs anything clarified before proceeding. Demonstrate – by your words *and* actions – that you truly are there to help.

Customs and Traditions

If you observe someone engaging in a tradition or custom you are unfamiliar with, learn about it. This will help you better serve your client and your company.

Remember that the accepted norms of our country could be in direct conflict with those of other cultures. For example, certain cultures are male dominant. If you are a woman selling to a man from a male dominant culture, give him time to know and respect you as a professional. That way, he will feel comfortable working with you. Remember, respect is a two-way street – you have to give it in order to get it.

Some cultures prefer making "family decisions." They will want to include all family members before making a major purchase. Don't let this frustrate you. Request an opportunity to speak with the entire family. Be patient and understanding.

Finally, avoid making judgments based on race, religion, gender, age, or color. Jokes or degrading comments relating to ethnic background, gender, and age are absolutely inappropriate in the workplace – or for that matter, *anywhere*. Remember, this country was founded on the principle that all men are created equal. We must understand and respect our differences in order to serve and sell in the global marketplace.

Personality and Behavioral Differences

Throughout your sales career, you will also deal with a wide array of personality types: direct, analytical, dominant, shy, defensive, sensitive, excitable, and intense – just to name a few. Keeping your emotions in check when negotiating with different personalities is another key to success.

We all know the value of having a high IQ. But are you aware of the immense value of possessing a high EQ (Emotional Intelligence)? Studies show that EQ is even more critical to your success than IQ.

Typically, someone with high emotional intelligence has a keen awareness and understanding of his or her own emotions and those of others. In general, being emotionally intelligent means that you can relate well with others. You are a better persuader because you are better at expressing your feelings and thoughts ... because you have empathy for differing points of view.

As a salesperson, you need to draw upon your emotional intelligence. Listen – not just to the words of your clients, but to your gut feelings as well. Be sensitive to the mood changes and the personality differences of your customers. Do your best to connect with their feelings regarding the sales transaction. When you respect and value differences in others, a special kind of trust is created ... a trust that will take you far beyond your current sales transaction.

Of course, at some point you will have a client who is boisterous and down right rude. Don't take it personally. Maintain your professionalism and you'll likely earn his or her respect.

You will also encounter clients who are timid – perhaps insecure about making a purchase. Focus on increasing their sense of security. Gear the sales presentation around how your product will help them be more successful.

In sales, as in life, you must learn to adapt to different types of people. Tune in to your emotions and the emotions of others. Win over a challenging customer and you'll have the best of all buyers.

Ethical Differences

Learning about your customer's values is a great way to understand him or her. Those values influence buying decisions. So exhibiting respect for different beliefs and values is crucial throughout the sales process.

However, there is one area for which you should have no tolerance: *unethical behavior.* If a customer asks you to do something that you know is inappropriate, STOP! Listen to your conscience. If it feels wrong, it probably *is* wrong. Give the customer an opportunity to "save face" and reconsider his or her requirements.

I appreciate your offer and I understand you want what's best for your company. So do I. Let's find another way to make this work for both of us.

When in doubt as to how to handle a difficult situation, seek advice from a manager or mentor. Remember, the *means* is as important as the *ends*. *How* you sell is as important as *how much* you sell! Never compromise your ethical standards to get a sale.

The ethical salesperson works hard to understand and embrace diversity in others. Expand your view of the world. Experience the joy of learning from others who are "different" from you. Have fun selling to *everyone!*

Be assured that you'll always have time for the things you put first."

~ Liane Steele

GIVE AND GET
YOUR MONEY'S WORTH

Throughout this book, we have discussed why it's critically important to behave in an ethical manner at all times. Most of the information presented has centered around your customer's needs. Yet, as a sales professional, you have other obligations – ethical obligations to your organization that go well beyond your selling responsibilities. Here are just a few of them:

Expense Privileges

It is essential that you use company property and privileges with great respect and discretion. Never abuse or misuse your expense account. It is your responsibility to be familiar with all expense guidelines provided by your organization. If your company does not have written guidelines, ask your manager for clarification before incurring expenses.

One way of assessing your expense boundaries is to think about how you would want your money spent if it was your company. Does your customer need a free coffee mug every time you visit, or is one enough? Was lunch with Aunt Liz really business related?

Do not assume expenses which were covered by your former employer will be covered by your current employer. Every organization is different and has different expectations. Review and abide by all company policies regarding entertaining clients and purchasing client gifts. But remember there may not be a policy for every situation. Use common sense and treat company assets with the utmost respect.

Proprietary Information

As a sales representative, you should receive advance notice of your company's upcoming product releases and up-to-the-minute product features. Be extra careful not to divulge confidential or proprietary information without authorization. It is important to verify, beforehand, what you are allowed to share with your customers. Releasing confidential information could end up being very costly for your organization.

Along with information about *your* company, you may also be privy to information regarding your *client's* company. Again, use discretion before sharing what you know. Information given to you in a meeting with a client should be kept confidential. Treat this inside knowledge with tremendous respect. Most importantly, never share a client's proprietary information with another client without permission.

Critical Feedback

What you can and should share with your organization is your customer's feedback regarding the services and products you are selling. As the sales representative, you will have the best opportunity to gain valuable insight from your customers. Your organization will count on you to pass along any knowledge you acquire about the changing needs of your marketplace. It is your responsibility to provide honest and direct feedback from your customers about your products and services. Do not assume that people in your company will receive this essential information via marketing research. They need to hear from *you* – the person with the most direct customer contact.

Keep track of which marketing pieces worked well and which pieces didn't. Make sure you ask your clients how they originally heard about your organization. Keep a log of customer comments and product complaints. Remember: when putting together client feedback, stay as objective as possible ... stick to the facts.

Succession Plan

You should also make sure that your company and your customer's will not lose a step should something happen to you. You owe it to those you work for and serve to create your own succession plan. Provide your clients with a secondary contact if they cannot reach you. Get in the habit of documenting all of your conversations, proposals, bids, and follow-up commitments. Be sure to show someone else how to obtain this information if you become unavailable. In your absence, it is important that others can pick up where you left off.

Time Is Money

If not adhered to, all of the issues mentioned above certainly could cost your organization an incredible amount of money. However, the most common cost abuse is a salesperson's misuse of time.

Think of your time as golden sand in an hour glass. Everything that you do (or don't do) is allowing precious gold to slip through the center. Once gone, you can't get it back. Time is the most valuable resource you and your company possess. To use it well, you have to be organized.

Salespeople know that if they spend too much time getting organized they won't have enough time to sell. While this is generally true, doing some initial, upfront organizing will allow for more "selling" time down the road.

75

If you have not created a tracing and filing system that allows you to easily track all of your contacts and correspondence, do it now! If your company does not offer an automated customer maintenance system, request one. If you need to do it manually, take the time to do it THIS WEEK!

Do you struggle with managing your time wisely? If so, take a time management class or read a book on the subject. Then, commit to *applying* your newly acquired knowledge. Staying organized – using your time efficiently – is a critical component of successful selling. The best time to start getting a handle on it is NOW!

Qualify, Quantify, or Quit!

Most salespeople have made the mistake of spending too much time with the wrong customer. Either they found out that their original point of contact was not the decision maker, or they discovered that the customer they were working with did not have the authority to make the purchase. No matter the reason, as soon as you realize that your contact is not the appropriate buyer, you will need to find the correct person – quickly! This can be a bit tricky. Continue to be respectful to the initial contact, but do your best to work directly with the decision maker.

It's best to **qualify** your customers early in the sales process. As part of a needs assessment, be sure to ask "qualifying questions" in the very beginning:

> *If we decide upon a suitable solution today, who will authorize the purchasing order?*

Asking these types of questions may feel awkward – even discourteous. But doing so is an important part of your job. Most likely, you will *never* uncover this information if you do not ask. Just make sure you're diplomatic and sensitive as you transition your activities to the decision maker:

In order for me to best help your company, it may be more efficient if I spoke to Ms. Jones directly. How can we arrange a meeting with her?

Along with qualifying your customer, you must also **quantify** each selling scenario. That means determining if each potential sale will be a profitable venture for your organization. Will your company be able to handle the needs and requirements of the job? Will your customer pay promptly? Have they hinted at special needs that may be cost-prohibitive? Does any discount in pricing impact your organization's ability to service the project?

As your selling career progresses, so should your expertise. You are expected to understand all of the dynamics that make a sales transaction successful … for everyone.

Unquestionably, the greatest misuse of time for salespeople is devoting too much time and attention to customers who are not going to buy. As soon as you know a customer does not need your product, it's time to **quit**. Direct him or her to another source as respectfully as possible. You will want to leave the door open for the customer to approach you if his or her situation changes. But, you must move on to find other prospects.

Getting Your Money's Worth

Remember you are a representative of your entire organization. Everyone is counting on you to be a symbol of your company's values. Being a professional and ethical salesperson means understanding all of the complex responsibilities that come with your position.

Make sure that you and your company are getting your money's worth. Stay committed to the agreements you have made with your customers, yourself, and your organization. Respect and value the company's time and resources – along with your own integrity.

SELL WITH ETHICS IN AN UNETHICAL WORLD

You probably wouldn't be reading this book if you didn't already have a desire to sell ethically. Congratulations! You have made the right choice. You are on your way to becoming a true sales professional. However, you wouldn't need this book if the road ahead was going to be easy and uncontested.

We live in a world comprised of people with different values and ethical beliefs. It is possible that you will encounter unethical coworkers, customers, and ... yes, even client managers and business owners. Each of those encounters brings pressure and opposition to your goal of selling with ethics. But those are pressures you can overcome. Not only is it possible to maintain your high ethical standards in a compromised working environment, but you can become the role model for others to follow.

Walk the Talk

Unfortunately, there are salespeople who truly believe that they have to lie or cheat in order to be successful. They may have been taught to sell unethically by a former employer. They may have worked at another organization that encouraged unethical behavior or simply looked the other way when it was happening.

The best thing you can do to encourage a more ethical culture in your organization is to *be* ethical yourself. Try to influence others by your example. When you consistently behave and sell ethically, others will notice and will want to follow in your footsteps.

Do your selling out in the open. Let your supervisors and coworkers know how you obtained the business. Let them observe your integrity-based sales methods. You don't have to be preachy to get your message across. The best way to let others know what beliefs and values are important to you is by *demonstrating* them!

Be the Catalyst!

Sell your colleagues on the idea of creating a more ethical culture in your organization. Let them know that organizations which foster ethical environments have higher employee retention rates, less employee turnover, and better morale. Sales professionals who work in organizations that are committed to high ethical standards take more pride in their work. They target more ethical customers and, therefore, get better sales results. Try not to come across as a know-it-all. Instead make it clear that you truly care about your company and want it to be the best it can be.

Stay away from blaming others. Instead, talk to your manager about any current practices that you believe are inappropriate and work together to come up with alternative approaches. If you believe that coworkers are performing unethically, address the issue. Privately share your viewpoint in a respectful and tactful manner:

I'm not sure if you are aware of it, however ...

I'm sure you meant no harm, but it really bothers me when ...

Once you have shared your perceptions, give them time to reflect on their behavior and the potential consequences. Focus on finding a better way for the future. Help them identify alternative means to accomplish their sales goals.

Know What's Uncompromisable!

Some aspects of selling are discretionary – you and your peers are given room to maneuver, compromise, and make deals within established boundaries. Some parts of business aren't discretionary – they're clear cut, black and white issues where compromise is unacceptable. And it's critically important that you understand what falls into which category.

While different organizations provide different operating latitude, there are several universal arenas where zero tolerance for violations is appropriate. These include: laws and regulations, public and employee safety, and truthfulness of records and statements. If you discover a violation in one of these areas, you may be tempted to "go along to get along." But that would be consciously doing what you believe is unethical – making you equally as wrong as the other person. Fight the temptation! Take a stand! Say NO … with tact.

State your objection and concern without indictment. Don't accuse the other person of being unethical. Instead, use "I statements" to describe your feelings:

I have serious concerns about that, and I need your understanding.
I believe it is wrong because … and I can't do what I believe is wrong.

Then, propose an alternative action that you feel is ethical:

I think I know what you want to accomplish, and I feel there is a better way to do it. How about ...

Finally, ask for the person's help and agreement:

I really need your help. I want to make sure we both do the right thing. Will you work with me on this one?

If the person does not agree, seek advice from an appropriate authority.

Extend the Olive Branch

Don't hold grudges. Nobody's perfect. We all make mistakes and we all, periodically, need to be given the benefit of the doubt. It is important to forgive coworkers and customers for past misbehaviors in order to begin a more promising future. Cut people the same slack you would want from them.

Talk *With* People – Not *About* Them

Don't use the unethical actions of others to justify your own inappropriate behavior – especially when it comes to *gossip*. Never say something be-hind someone's back that you haven't already told him or her face-to-face. As difficult as this can be, it is crucial that you directly communicate your concerns. By gossiping with others, you lessen the chances of actually helping those with problems change their behaviors.

Stay the Course

Encouraging a more ethical culture in your workplace is an admirable goal worth fighting for. However, it is not going to happen overnight! There will be areas that are out of your control. Have patience with the process, and have compassion for the perspectives of others.

Don't strive for perfection. Instead, work toward improvement. Use diplomacy and discretion. And most importantly, NEVER GIVE UP!

Success is the sum of small efforts
repeated day-in and day-out.

~ Robert Collier

MASTER THE SECRETS
OF SUCCESS

Different organizations and industries will require different selling proc-
esses and sales cycles. And different salespeople will operate with special
and unique selling styles. Regardless of those differences, ethics and integrity must be at the core of every sales endeavor. They are, after all, *the*
critical components of success. However, along with ethics and integrity,
there are several other behaviors that are common to most successful
salespeople. These distinguishing traits will help you establish and maintain your own successful sales career:

1. Discipline Yourself. All of the top-notch sellers I know are self-
disciplined. They understand that maintaining a successful career requires
hard work. Professional salespeople are not disillusioned about getting the
"one lucky break." They're willing to sweat.

These hard-working individuals typically need very little supervision because they manage themselves. They do what is required without the
need of bosses looking over their shoulders. They stay mentally and emotionally tough. They often come in early and stay late so they can be
ahead of the game. They study product brochures, competitors' websites,
and industry trends – without being asked.

They know what it takes to get the job done ... and they do it!

Hard work spotlights the character of people:
some turn up their sleeves, some turn up their noses,
and some don't turn up at all.

~ Sam Ewig

2. Learn from Mistakes. Great salespeople didn't become that way overnight. They were just like other people in the beginning of their careers. They made a fair amount of mistakes when they first started – and they continue to make mistakes as seasoned veterans. Unlike other people, however, they chose to use their mistakes as learning opportunities to help ensure a better future ... and they still do!

Everybody makes an occasional mistake. Don't expect your selling career to run perfectly. What's critically important is that you ask yourself: *What will I do differently next time? How can I improve my presentation, my listening skills, my communication skills, my needs analysis, etc.*

Don't blame your mistakes on external circumstances such as the economy, your industry, or your customers. Be personally accountable. Acknowledge your mistakes and learn from them. Ask coworkers to critique your sales presentations and be grateful for constructive feedback. More importantly, use it! This will help you enjoy a career that continues to improve and excel.

Prosperity is a great teacher; adversity is a greater one.

~ William Hazlitt

3. Embrace Change. Successful salespeople thrive on change. They understand the importance of modifying their presentations for various buyer types. They know they must adjust their sales tactics as the economy and industry change. They don't expect the sales strategies that helped them excel in yesterday's market to be as effective today.

Not only is it essential that you adapt to the changing needs of your customers and your industry, but you also must look for trends or signals offering clues as to how you'll need to adjust your sales approach in the future. Be proactive. Be a front-runner! Rather than aiming to keep up with the current pace, *set* the pace for others to follow.

Do not follow where the path may lead. Go instead
where there is no path and leave a trail.

~ Unknown

4. Motivate Yourself. Just about every salesperson wants to be at his or her best. But being your best, all of the time, is a tall order. You must motivate yourself ... every day.

Top sellers have the ability to pick themselves up when they get knocked down. They don't take rejection personally. They don't procrastinate. They don't whine or complain. They do not allow themselves to get caught up in petty gossip or any senseless negativity that may be exhibited by their peers.

Successful salespeople monitor what they're feeling *and* what they're saying to themselves. They quickly eliminate negative thoughts that can drain their energy. They focus on positive and encouraging self-talk.

When they feel down or lethargic, they go for a brisk walk or read an up-lifting, motivational book. They take responsibility for their attitudes.

Keep your thoughts optimistic and upbeat. Stay fresh. Be your own cheerleader. Control your skepticism. See the glass half-full rather than half-empty. Find nuggets of inspiration in your daily routines that will give you the motivation you need to persevere.

Human beings, by changing the inner attitudes of their minds, can change the outer aspects of their lives.

~ William James

5. Care for Customers. Throughout this book there has been continued emphasis on focusing on the needs of the customer. Because this is so critical, I feel obliged to say it one more time: Customers come first.

In sales, you will feel pressure from many different avenues. You will have internal organizational pressures, financial pressures, peer pressures – and of course, pressures from your customers. Remember that, if you want a successful selling career, nothing is more important than your customers.

Putting the customer first sounds simple – but it can be harder than some people think. It's not unusual to get caught up in the various demands that are pulling at you. These demands can take away from your ability to focus on the people you're there to serve. Think "customer first" when prioritizing your day. When planning your activities, determine which tasks will impact your customer the most … and then DO THEM!

Successful salespeople value their customers' perspectives over their own. They don't underestimate their clients' intelligence. They regularly follow up with their customers to make sure they stay connected.

Your organization is counting on you to be the advocate for its clients. Putting customers first is the best way to ensure prosperity for your business and yourself.

Customer service doesn't come from a manual;
it comes from the heart!

~ Debbie ("Mrs.") Fields

6. Have Pride in Your Work. Top-notch salespeople take pride in every aspect of their careers. They are proud of the company they represent; they are proud of the product they sell. They are especially proud of their selling achievements because they know what it took to get them.

There is no need to boast or brag about your accomplishments. But it is important you take pride in what you do. Bring your best to the workplace each and every day. Be confident. Taking pride in your work and doing your best means you'll never have regrets. Never settle for mediocrity or it will settle you.

The man who has confidence in himself
gains the confidence of others.

~ Hasidic Saying

7. Stay Focused on Goals. Top sellers understand the importance of setting and achieving goals. Naturally, they establish long-term, annual sales goals and personal objectives. But they also institute short-term goals that will channel them towards their longer-term ambitions. They utilize daily goals to keep themselves consistent and focused. (I actually know salespeople who will not take a morning coffee break until they have accomplished a few "mini-targets" that they set for themselves.)

A salesperson's goals should be clear and specific ... realistic yet challenging. Write your goals down and keep them in front of you. Evaluate them regularly to see how you are doing. Envision yourself accomplishing your goals, and allow yourself to enjoy the feeling of success. Finally, be sure to celebrate your achievements.

Obstacles are those frightful things you see when
you take your eyes off your goals.

~ Ralph Waldo Emerson

8. Maintain a Sense of Purpose. Professional salespeople understand that it's not enough to sell a product or service for financial gain alone. To maintain long-term success, your selling career must offer you a sense of purpose, as well. You must feel good about what you sell.

For example: if you sell minivans, focus on how minivans benefit the families that buy them. If you sell pencils, center your thoughts on the students that will use the pencils for learning.

To be sure, most of us are "in sales" to earn a living. However, earning that living is much more gratifying when we understand how our products make a positive impact on the lives of others. The good feelings that you will derive from having a sense of purpose will allow you to put your heart and soul into your career. And doing that will positively impact your selling results.

Real success is finding your lifework in the work that you love.

~ David McCullough

9. Take Ownership. Salespeople who enjoy a high level of success year-after-year do so because they have a mindset of ownership. They take complete ownership of their sales objectives – along with the relationships they maintain with their customers. They don't grumble about unfair sales goals. They don't complain that they have "bad" customers. They understand their responsibilities; they choose to own the sales process and be accountable for the outcome.

Take responsibility for your career. Don't blame others for your failures. If you are disappointed with the outcome, evaluate how you can improve in the future. And when you succeed, pat yourself on the back for a job well done.

You cannot escape the responsibility of tomorrow
by evading it today.

~ Abraham Lincoln

10. L⌐ ... ⌐f a sales representative for any organization

⌐ times (especially at the end of the

⌐ou could cut it with a knife. You will

⌐o overwhelm you.

⌐y definitely is underrated. Laughter is a great

⌐ get on with your job. Laughter will help you

⌐lear and fresh. Laughing gives you energy and

⌐ will allow you to better connect with others. Laugh-

⌐ good!

⌐y far the most significant activity of the human brain.

~ Edward De Bono

11. Seize Opportunities. Opportunity is a gift that creates anxiety in some people and jubilation in others. Top sellers see opportunities throughout each day. These individuals turn challenges into chances. They understand that the client who doesn't need the product today may know of someone who does tomorrow. They know that the customer who presented an objection last month might change his or her mind next month.

Upon first glance, most opportunities are deceiving – some appearing risky or unobtainable. This can lead many salespeople to dismissing potential ventures without enough consideration. You must allow yourself time to envision the possibilities.

Seizing opportunities rarely is easy. It typically requires a lot of hard work. Don't be afraid of what might *not* happen. Instead, stay focused on the potential, and you will see more opportunities in front of you.

> *Opportunity is missed by most people because it is dressed in overalls and looks like work.*
>
> ~ Thomas Edison

12. Express Your Passion! Finally, successful salespeople have passion. They have passion for their products, the services they provide, their customers, their professionalism, and their integrity.

It's passion that motivates sellers to make one more call. It's passion that drives them to rewrite a proposal. It's passion that encourages them to follow up with their clients. Passion gives them energy that spills over into everything they do. They love their work and they have fun selling. As a result, people want to buy from them.

Don't inhibit your passion at work. Love what you do and let it show. Express your passion for your product and your customers with enthusiasm. Passion is contagious. Let it loose!

> *Nothing great in the world has ever been accomplished without passion.*
>
> ~ G. W. F. Hegel

The Secret is YOU!

There is no other profession quite like selling. It requires a unique individual who has a driven yet compassionate spirit.

That individual is YOU!

You make the difference. *You* are the secret to your success. *You* have chosen a noble profession. Enjoy it!

A CLOSING STORY

It was a warm September afternoon in 1973. My brothers, sisters, and I were impatiently waiting for mom to pick us up from school. I can see her pull around the corner in the green Ford station wagon – smiling and waving until she sees that each of us has several boxes of *World's Finest Chocolate Bars* sitting on our laps. A look of despair suddenly appears on her face. She is well aware of the chaos that is about to hit our household.

You see, we attended The Sacred Heart Academy. And every year, *World's Finest Chocolates* were part of a massive fundraiser for destitute children in third-world countries. My three brothers, two sisters, and I would desperately try to sell every bar of chocolate we could in order to help the poor, starving children throughout the world. And, of course, there were prizes. *World's Finest Chocolate Company* offered incredible rewards for selling higher quantities of chocolate bars.

If you sold two boxes (ten bars in each box for $1.00 a bar) you would qualify for a "Level A prize" which typically consisted of routine items such as jump ropes, key chains, coloring books, and stickers. Nothing worth drooling over! "Level B" was reached after you sold a minimum of three boxes. Once again the items were fairly unimpressive. But, just a step higher – if you somehow managed to sell more than four boxes – you would immediately qualify for "Level C"! Level C offered a selection of really cool stuff: roller skates, super squirt guns, and a portable AM radio. The radio was what I had my eye on. It was bright neon pink and small enough to fit in my backpack. *Very cool!*

Here were the rules for selling in the Correia house: The names of relatives would be placed in a bowl and we would draw from it. You could only sell to the relatives you drew. My mom didn't want all of her kids harassing our entire extended family. (One call would be bad enough!) We were also allowed to sell door-to-door within a one-mile radius of our house. "You can't go past the Food Basket or the Little League Field," Mom would say. (Little did I know I had just received my first sales territory!)

We all knew the most coveted family member to draw was my grandmother – or as we called her in Portuguese, "Vovo." Vovo was the easiest person to sell to because she had a hard time saying no to her grandchildren. Besides, she genuinely cared about poor children. As luck would have it, this was my year ... I pulled Vovo's name. I could already hear the music from my new portable radio.

I decided not to call Vovo on the phone. I thought I would be much more effective if I visited her in person. So, I hopped on my bike and pedaled four blocks to her house.

As usual, Vovo was in the kitchen baking sweet bread. She laughed as I opened the door with my box of chocolates. "It won't be as easy this year," she said with a smile. "I don't have much money. But I *will* help you out."

She proceeded to tell me that she would match whatever I sold on my own. So, if I sold ten bars, she would buy ten. "I won't buy anything until you sell some on your own," she uttered, as she watched me ride down the driveway.

I left my grandmother's house terribly disappointed. I thought for sure that she would buy all of the forty bars I needed to earn the neon pink radio. Now what? I realized, then and there, that I had two choices: give up and forget about the radio or go door-to-door until I sold at least twenty bars. I chose to go for it.

September can be the hottest month of the year in San Diego because of the Santa Ana winds. And this particular week was evidence of that. It was hot – really hot! Riding from house to house was hard work – but not as tough as keeping the chocolates from melting.

I remember visiting one house where a man asked me why I was selling the chocolate. "To get a really cool radio!" I replied. He didn't buy anything. I quickly realized he was looking for a more noble cause like helping poor children. As I thought about those kids, I began to feel very selfish. "Here I am worrying about a silly radio while there are children who don't even have food to eat!" It dawned on me how self-centered I had become. I was frustrated with my grandmother for not buying all the chocolates outright. And, I was mad at *myself* for not caring about the real reason for the fundraiser.

Somehow, I managed to sell twenty bars that Friday afternoon. I achieved my goal and still had my weekend free. I was very pleased with myself as I called Vovo to advise her of my results. As we talked, I could hear the concern in her voice. "Oh my, I didn't realize that you would sell so many. Twenty dollars is a lot of money for me right now. But I did make a promise. Come by tomorrow and I will give you the money. I want to help the children," she said in her heavy Portuguese accent.

That night, as I tossed and turned in bed, I thought about my grandmother. She was such a nice lady. She was so honest and good. I shouldn't take her money. But what about the poor children? They needed it. I could easily justify taking Vovo's money. But deep down I knew I should try harder to sell the additional chocolates needed to win the radio without my grandmother's help.

I spent the rest of the weekend selling candy. My brothers and sisters had given up. They were too hot ... and the prizes were not as attractive as the television in the family room. Interestingly enough, as I stopped thinking about the radio and focused on the poor children, the work became more satisfying. When I told people why I was selling the chocolates, I was proud of my efforts. I think my customers could feel my noble intentions. They could sense I genuinely cared about others. I also understood that they wanted to feel good about helping poor children – not about helping me earn a radio. When I sincerely focused on what they wanted, I had no trouble selling all forty chocolate bars by Sunday afternoon.

The best part was when I stopped by Vovo's house to let her know that she didn't have to buy any of the chocolate. She was proud of me. She told me I could sell to her for the next fundraiser – even if I didn't draw her name. I could sell to her anytime. I had gained her trust. Gaining Vovo's trust was priceless.

So what is the moral of this story? Sure, that weekend I learned that I was good at selling. I also found out that hard work pays off. I learned that I needed to care about the needs of my customers before my own. By focusing on their needs, I would earn their trust. And that would help me get what I needed. Most importantly, I learned that when I sell with integrity, I feel good about myself – and others feel good about buying from me.

As an adult, I went on to enjoy a rather lucrative selling career. I made many mistakes along the way. But as I look back, I realize that my biggest mistakes occurred when I put my own needs in front of my customers.

Choosing a career in sales is great way to make a living. Choosing to sell with ethics and integrity is not only good for you, it's good for your customers. Don't think about what you can *get* from the people you serve. Instead, focus on what you can *give* to them. Treat every customer with the respect and compassion you would if he or she was a member of your own family.

By selling it right, you will not only earn a paycheck, you will earn your customer's respect. When you have customers that trust and respect you, you have customers ... for life.

THE AUTHOR

Michelle Correia Templin is a renowned speaker, author, and business consultant. For over twenty years, Michelle has been conducting high-energy workshops that motivate and inspire attendees. She is a firm believer that learning should be passionate and purposeful!

Michelle has hands-on, successful selling experience in a wide array of industries – banking, hospitality, retail, and manufacturing. She has negotiated multi-million dollar contracts internationally and effectively led Domestic and International Sales Teams.

Michelle has worked with several renowned authors including, Dr. Spencer Johnson, author of *Who Moved My Cheese?*, Dr. Stephen Covey, author of *The Seven Habits of Highly Effective People*, and Eric Harvey, author of *Ethics4Everyone*.

Ms. Correia Templin studied at the University of San Diego under the direction of Robert Austin. She is President of Get Smart Training, Inc and a member of the San Diego Leadership Initiative. Michelle resides in La Costa, California with her husband and three energetic children.

WALK THE TALK® Presentations & Workshops

Bring Michelle Correia Templin and her powerful message to your organization through our high-impact:

- ✔ Keynote & Conference Presentations
- ✔ Leadership Development Workshops
- ✔ Train-The-Trainer/Certification Services

WALK THE TALK Presentations and Workshops are customized to your audience, organizational culture, and targeted business objectives. Our cadre of experienced authors and facilitators are dedicated to providing you with a powerful educational experience, to help you ensure the complete success of your sponsored event.

We offer educational programs and presentations on each topic covered in our best selling books to include:

- Selling and Goal Setting Techniques
- Effective Leadership Techniques
- Business Ethics and Values Alignment
- Coaching and Performance Improvement Strategies
- Building Customer Service Attitudes and Behaviors
- Techniques to Attract and Retain "The Best and Brightest Employees"
- Building a High-Performance Culture
- Dealing With Organizational Change
- And much, much more

To learn more:

 Call 972.243.8863 or toll free 800.888.2811

or

 Email info@walkthetalk.com

Introducing the WALK THE TALK®

Sales Success Tool Kit!

The perfect tool to help ALL your sales people become more successful!

Contains the following publications:

Selling It Right
Goal Setting For Results
Listen Up, Sales and Customer Service
180 Ways to Walk the Customer Service Talk
136 Effective Presentation Tips
Get In the Game

ONLY $49.95!

Order today!

www.walkthetalk.com

Toll Free: 888.822.9255
or

Fax the completed order form to 972.243.0815

*Want to build **Selling It Right!** skills with your team? Well...we now have the answer for you!*

Introducing the

Selling It Right!
UTRAIN
Program

Whether you are a team leader, manager or seasoned training professional, UTrain Programs provide the resources you need to turn information into action. Each program provides a variety of delivery options, exercises and techniques which can be customized to fit your timetable, group size, and organizational goals.

UTrain programs include a full range of high-impact resources:

✓ Leaders Guide with instructions, learning exercises, preparation suggestions, and other training tips.

✓ Comprehensive participant materials to include "back-on-the-job" reminder resources.

✓ PowerPoint training visuals which can easily be customized to fit your audience and training objectives.

For only **$79.95**, you can train your entire team on the **Selling It Right!** key concepts. Once you order, you will receive instructions via email on how to download the complete **Selling It Right! UTrain Program**. It's that easy! Please make sure you include your email address on the order form when you order. Better yet, order online at www.walkthetalk.com and download immediately!

The Walk The Talk Company

Since 1977, **The WALK THE TALK® Company** has helped organizations, worldwide, achieve success through Ethical Leadership and Values-Based Business Practices. And our team of experienced professionals is ready to do the same ... for YOU!

We offer the following professional services:

- Keynote and Conference Presentations
- Customized Workshops
- Executive Retreats
- Consulting Services
- "How To" Handbooks
- Video Training Packages
- *and much more!*

To learn more:

Call: 1.888.822.9255

E-mail: info@walkthetalk.com

Visit: www.walkthetalk.com

ORDER FORM

Have questions? Need assistance? Call **1.888.822.9255**

☑ **Please send me more copies of Selling It Right!**

1-24 copies $12.95 each   25-99 copies $11.95 each   100-499 copies $10.95 each

Selling It Right!	_____ copies X _____	=$ _____
Selling It Right UTRAIN Program	_____ copies X $79.95	=$ _____
Selling It Right! Success Tool Kit	_____ sets X $49.95	=$ _____

Client Priority Code

503SM

(Sales & Use Tax Collected on TX & CA Customers Only)

Product Total	$ _____
*Shipping & Handling	$ _____
Subtotal	$ _____
Sales Tax:	
Texas Sales Tax – 8.25%	$ _____
CA Sales/Use Tax	$ _____
Total (U.S. Dollars Only)	$ _____

*Shipping and Handling Charges

No. of Items	1-4	5-9	10-24	25-49	50-99	100-199	200+
Total Shipping	$6.75	$10.95	$17.95	$26.95	$48.95	$84.95	$89.95+$0.25/book

Call 972.243.8863 for quote if outside continental U.S. Orders are shipped ground delivery 7-10 days. Next and 2nd business day delivery available – call 888.822.9255.

Name_____ Title_____

Organization_____

Shipping Address_____

City_____ (No PO Boxes) State_____ Zip_____

Phone_____ Fax_____

E-Mail (required for UTRAIN orders):_____

Charge Your Order: ❑ MasterCard   ❑ Visa   ❑ American Express

Credit Card Number_____ Exp. Date_____

❑ Check Enclosed (Payable to The WALK THE TALK Company)

❑ Please Invoice (**Orders over $250 ONLY**)   ❑ P.O. Number (if applicable)_____

PHONE	**FAX**	**MAIL**
1.888.822.9255	972-243-0815	WALK THE TALK Co.
or 972.243.8863	**ONLINE**	2925 LBJ Fwy., #201
M-F, 8:30-5:00 Cen.	www.walkthetalk.com	Dallas, TX 75234

Prices effective January 2005 are subject to change.